C000153028

Ohio Images

**Photographs by
J. Miles Wolf**

Columbus, Ohio

Copyright c 2003 J.Miles Wolf
All rights reserved under International and Pan-American Copyright Conventions. No part of this book may be reproduced in any form or by any electronic or mechanical means without permission in writing from the publisher.
ISBN-0-9647433-6-1

Wolf Publishing Company
2165 Gilbert Avenue
Cincinnati, OH 45206
513-281-6555
www.jmileswolf.com

Captions by: Julie Irwin
Design and Layout by: Mariesa Conmay
Printed in Canada

Ohio has it all! From quaint little country towns to major metropolitan cities, from the Ohio River to Lake Erie, there are millions of interesting people, places and buildings to visit. This collection of photographs represents 25 years of traveling the back roads, exploring the little towns and seeking out the natural wonders of the state.

In 2003, The State of Ohio is celebrating its 200th birthday. This milestone will be marked by special Bicentennial events around the entire state, from cultural activities in the major cities to glimpses of Ohio's past in its small towns and rural countryside.

I was born in Ohio, and I love living here today. It is my pleasure to share these images with you. I hope it awakens your curiosity and convinces you to get out and explore some of what Ohio has to offer.

J. Miles Wolf

Hocking Hills

This region, located in central Ohio near Athens, is part of the Wayne National Forest. Hikers, campers, fishermen and horseback riders enjoy the outdoors in the area's nine state parks and more than 9,000 acres of state forestland. Attractions include **Cedar Falls**, a hiking trail in **Conkle's Hollow**, and **Old Man's Cave**.

Pumpkin gathering on a farm near Circleville, Ohio, just south of Columbus. The Circleville Pumpkin Show attracts hundreds of thousands of visitors to the annual event.

Serpent Mound, in Adams County, is a prehistoric effigy mound shaped like a snake with its mouth open. Much about the quarter-mile-long mound remains a mystery, but it is believed that the Adena people built it about 2,000-3,000 years ago for religious or ceremonial events.

Agriculture

Agriculture is the top industry in Ohio, generating about $73 billion per year. One in every six Ohio residents is employed in some aspect of the industry, including farm production, wholesaling and retailing, marketing and processing, and agribusiness.

9

Tobacco air-drying in a barn in southwest Ohio. In 2001, more than 500 small tobacco farms in Ohio disappeared, and the heart of Ohio's tobacco belt has watched its crop shrink by half.

Harvesting wheat on an Ohio farm. Corn and soybeans are the leading crops, and Ohio leads the nation in the production of both Swiss cheese and eggs.

On Ohio's back roads, travelers can catch a glimpse of cattle grazing in fields. Nearly 400 acres of farmland disappear every day.

Sunrise, **Highland County.**

The **Little Miami River** in southwestern Ohio, once home to countless Indian villages that flourished along the banks, now welcomes fishing and canoeing enthusiasts to its scenic shores.

Columbus

Ohio's largest city as well as its capital, Columbus attracts visitors from around the world who enjoy its museums, sporting events and universities.
A full-sized replica of Christopher Columbus' ship the *Santa Maria* is moored in the Scioto River downtown, giving visitors a glimpse of what life was like for sailors 500 years ago.

The **Ohio Statehouse**, built in the 1860's, is one of the oldest working state capitals in the U.S. and one of the country's best examples of Greek Revival civic architecture.

Columbus' new **Nationwide Arena** is home ice to the NHL Blue Jackets. The arena also hosts special events and music concerts.

Columbus' **German Village** is one of the premier historic restoration projects in the world, with more than 1,600 buildings renovated since 1960. It is a thriving community that boasts a mix of homes, businesses, restaurants and bars.

Visitors to the **Franklin Park Conservatory & Botanical Garden** can wander through a tropical rain forest, an arid desert, and a cool Himalayan mountain – all within the historic 19th-century structure.

Ohio State University, one of the nation's largest universities, has 48,000 students enrolled at the Columbus campus. **The Wexner Art Center**, shown above, hosts gallery shows, performances and art films.

COSI, Columbus' famous Center of Science and Industry, uses multi-media, hands-on exhibits to make learning about science fun for visitors of all ages.

Autumn

Clear days and cold, crisp nights define the fall season in Ohio. The trees light up with color, and it's a great time to head to the countryside. Fields of grass are rolled into hay bails to feed the livestock over the winter.

Whether it's an overnight camping trip, an all-day fishing expedition or an hour-long hike, Ohio offers a vast range of outdoor recreation throughout the state. The changing seasons and varied topography add even greater variety to the mix of activities.

Clifton Gorge was formed millions of years ago, when meltwater from a receding glacier broke through limestone and shale, exposing dolomite that eventually collapsed. This National Natural Landmark encompasses a two-mile stretch of the Little Miami National Scenic River.

Historic Clifton Mill, perched above Clifton Gorge on the Little Miami River, is one of the largest water-powered gristmills still in existence. During the 1800s, more than 70 mills were located in surrounding Greene County; today Clifton Mill is the lone survivor of that once-prosperous industry.

Thanks to Ohio's Bicentennial barn-painting project, the Bicentennial logo appears on at least one barn in each of Ohio's 88 counties. This barn from the 1800's is in Pike County.

McCafferty Covered Bridge in Brown County, built in 1877, crosses the East Fork of the Little Miami River. Ohio once had almost 3,500 covered bridges; only a few more than 100 are still standing.

At **Sharon Woods**, the oldest park in the Hamilton County Park District, visitors can play in an Ice Age-themed water park, learn about the geological evolution of the area, tour 19th-century homes or simply enjoy some solitude in the park's 755 acres.

Hueston Woods

A remnant of the beech-maple forest that once stretched from southwest Ohio all the way to the northeast, **Hueston Woods** offers a 200-acre old-growth forest, boating and fishing on Acton Lake, and diverse wildlife populations. Overnight guests can camp or stay at the resort lodge, and indoor attractions include the **Pioneer Farm House and Museum** (right).

Golden Lamb

Past visitors to the **Golden Lamb** include Mark Twain, Harriet Beecher Stowe, Charles Dickens and a dozen U.S. presidents who have either eaten or slept at Ohio's oldest hotel. Opened in 1803 in Lebanon, the Golden Lamb serves up hearty, Shaker-style fare along with a glimpse into history. Nearby stands the station for the historic Turtle Creek and Lebanon Railway.

The city of **Hamilton** first appeared on the map in 1791 as Fort Hamilton, a frontier outpost on the east bank of the Great Miami River. Its proximity to the water gave rise to its first industries, textile and paper, and the great waves of German immigrants who arrived in the 1830s and 1840s led to a rapid industrial expansion.

The **Ohio River** runs 981 miles, from Pittsburgh, Pennsylvania to Cairo, Illinois. Once the main route to the newly opened West, the Ohio still carries barge traffic across its broad waters, along with recreational boats and the occasional steamwheeler.

Cincinnati

The riverfront, is in the midst of a massive renovation that celebrates its history and welcomes its future. Projects include the Cincinnati Central Riverfront Park, the Bengal's Paul Brown Stadium, the Red's Great American Ballpark, and the National Underground Railroad Freedom Center. The works complement development across the river in Northern Kentucky and in Cincinnati's downtown and neighborhoods.

The **John A. Roebling Suspension Bridge** spans the Ohio River from Covington, Kentucky to Cincinnati, Ohio. Built between 1856 and 1866, this bridge was the prototype for the Brooklyn Bridge. At the time of its opening, it was the longest bridge in the world.

Cincinnati Union Terminal was built as a train station in 1933. This wonderful art-deco building in now called the Cincinnati Museum Center, is home to the Cincinnati History Museum, the Museum of Natural History and the Cinergy Children's Museum.

Over the Rhine, a historic neighborhood next to downtown Cincinnati. Settled by German immigrants in the mid-1800's this area now draws locals and sightseers with its mix of bars, coffeeshops, galleries and antique stores.

In addition to its walking paths and picturesque overlooks, **Eden Park** is home to the Cincinnati Art Museum, Cincinnati Art Academy, Playhouse in the Park, Murray Seasongood Pavilion, and the Krohn Conservatory (above).

The narrow, hilly streets of the **Mt Adams** neighborhood, packed with a mix of houses, restaurants and bars, remind visitors of San Francisco. Its breathtaking views and proximity to downtown make it a popular choice for newly arrived young professionals.

Cincinnati's new football stadium, **Paul Brown Stadium**, opened in 2000. It is home to the NFL Bengals.

Whether it's the Bengals on a chilly Sunday, the Reds on a lazy summer afternoon or the fierce basketball rivalry between the University of Cincinnati and Xavier University, sports is a serious business in Cincinnati.

Every four years, Cincinnati celebrates its rich river history with **Tall Stacks**, a five-day event that recalls the romantic period in American history when rivers were the nation's highways. The 2003 Tall Stacks will feature at least 17 steamboats and a festival emphasizing the music, arts, and heritage that blossomed along the rivers. Participating steamers will include the legendary *Delta Queen*, the only authentic, fully restored, overnight steamboat in the world. It will mark the fifth consecutive Tall Stacks appearance for the *Delta Queen*.

Set amid rolling plains, **Highland County** is rich in natural resources and steeped in the Indian history of Ohio. Its picturesque courthouse (left) in the county seat of Hillsboro is the oldest courthouse still in use in Ohio. **Rocky Fork Lake** (right) is a paradise for outdoor enthusiasts. Great blue herons thrive in the wooded shorelines surrounding Rocky Fork Lake.

Dayton

The history of aviation is on display in **Dayton**, from the Wright Cycle Co., where Wilbur and Orville Wright developed their ideas that led to the invention of powered flight, to the United States Air Force Museum, which features over 300 aircraft and missiles and thousands of aviation artifacts. Universities, sports events and a thriving arts scene round out the city's attractions.

Marblehead Lighthouse, the oldest lighthouse in continuous operation on the Great Lakes, has guided sailors safely along the rocky shores of Lake Erie's Marblehead Peninsula since 1822. Of the 15 lighthouse keepers who have tended the beacon, two have been women, including Rachel Wolcott, widow of the first keeper Benjamin Wolcott.

Lake Erie is the smallest of the Great Lakes in volume, and its basin is the most densely populated of the five. Much of its southern shore was at one time occupied by the Eries, a tribe of Indians from which the lake derived its name.

Visitors to Kelleys Island, the largest American island in Lake Erie, can tour the 1860s **Kelley Mansion**. Accessible by ferry, private boat or airplane, Kelleys Island is a popular summer destination, when the population swells from 350 to more than 1,500.

Glacial grooves in **Kelleys Island State Park**, left more than 10,000 years ago by retreating Ice Age glaciers.

The horse-drawn buggy is the best-known symbol of the Amish and Mennonite people, who choose to live without electricity and automobiles. Known as the "plain people" because of their unadorned clothing, they speak "Pennsylvania Dutch" and generally avoid contact with strangers.

Cleveland

Once derided as the "mistake by the lake," Cleveland has engineered a turnaround that has made it a model of urban rebirth.

Since 1984, developers have pumped more than $1 billion into downtown, funding projects that include the Rock and Roll Hall of Fame and Museum (below); Tower City Center; Gateway Stadium and Gund Arena; Playhouse Square Center; and the Great Lakes Museum of Science and Technology.

View of the Cleveland Skyline from The Flats, a downtown entertainment district.

Since opening in 1994, **Jacobs Field** has sold out nearly 90 percent of its games, including a major League Baseball record 455 consecutive sellouts. The park, an intimate facility in the heart of downtown, combines modern luxuries with the features of classic ballparks.

An autumn scene along the tree-lined streets just outside Cleveland.

The **Fayette County Courthouse**, built in the late 19th century, is on the National Register of Historic Places. The courthouse is located in the city of Washington Court House, so named to separate the city from other towns with the same name in the state.

Maumee Bay in Toledo, on the southwest corner of Lake Erie. A port since before its 1837 founding, **Toledo** is
now one of the most diverse and productive ports along the Great Lakes St. Lawrence Seaway system.
Nearly half of Seaway traffic travels to and from overseas ports, especially in Europe, the Middle East and Africa.